The
Library
of Future
Medicine

The Revolution in
Medical Imaging

BARBARA MOE

The Rosen Publishing Group, Inc.
New York

The author is grateful to the following consultants:
Paul Moe, M.D., professor of pediatrics, The Children's Hospital, Denver, Colorado; Linda Murray, B.S. in radiology technology, technical director, Mae Boettcher Center for Pediatric Imaging, The Children's Hospital, Denver, Colorado; John Strain, M.D., professor and chairman, Department of Radiology, The Children's Hospital, Denver, Colorado; and Gordon Teubner, Associate of Arts in Applied Science and PACS coordinator, Mae Boettcher Center for Pediatric Imaging, The Children's Hospital, Denver, Colorado.

Published in 2003 by The Rosen Publishing Group, Inc.
29 East 21st Street, New York, NY 10010

Copyright © 2003 by The Rosen Publishing Group, Inc.

First Edition

Library of Congress Cataloging-in-Publication Data
Moe, Barbara.
The revolution in medical imaging / by Barbara Moe.— 1st ed.
    v. cm. — (The Library of future medicine)
Summary: Discusses the increasing use of scanning and diagnostic tools such as CAT, PET, and MRI to uncover the source and possible treatment of various medical problems.
Includes bibliographical references and index.
Contents: Chapter 1: X-Ray and Computer Technology Chapter 2: Plain Radiography Chapter 3: Tomography Chapter 4: Nuclear Medicine Chapter 5: Ultrasound Chapter 6: The Future of Medical Imaging Glossary: Bibliography and Index.
ISBN 0-8239-3672-4 (lib. bdg.)
1. Diagnostic imaging—Juvenile literature. [1. Diagnostic imaging.]
I. Title. II. Series.
RC78.7.D53 M64 2003
616'.0754—dc21

                                                          2002004155

Manufactured in the United States of America

Cover image: Doctors position a patient for radiographic imaging of the coronary arteries.

Contents

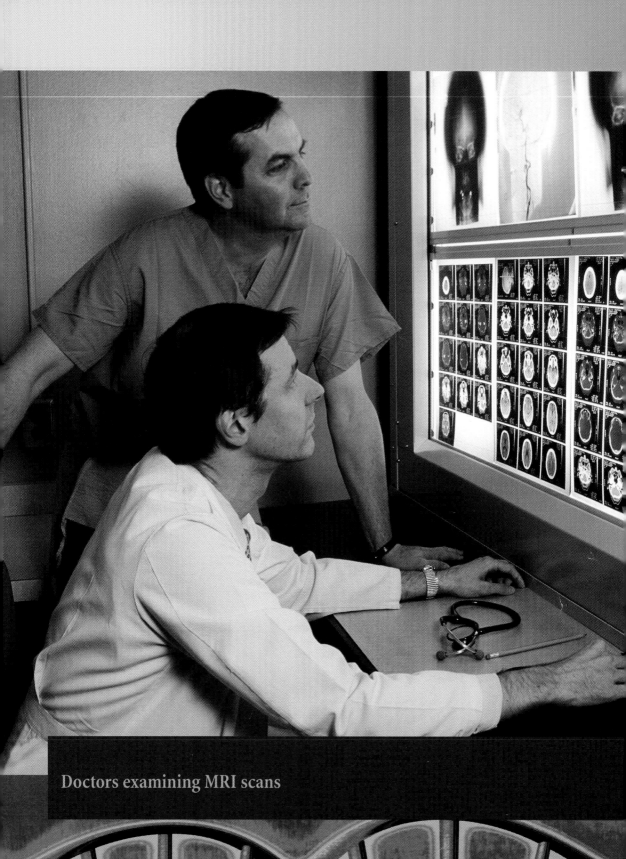

Doctors examining MRI scans

X-Ray and Computer Technology

Medical imaging started at the end of the nineteenth century with the X-ray. X-rays are powerful beams of electromagnetic energy that we cannot see, but which can penetrate the soft tissues of the body. When a photographic plate is placed on the other side of the body, X-rays produce a valuable picture of what's inside the body. Other imaging techniques followed over the next hundred years. They have allowed us to visualize what used to be inaccessible. They help doctors diagnose problems inside the body, such as broken bones, tumors, and torn muscles and ligaments.

Today, diagnostic imaging allows doctors to do preventive screening tests. It also helps doctors make a diagnosis without having to perform surgery to see what's wrong. Experts say 15 percent of this country's health-care dollar is spent on diagnostic imaging.

Today's diagnostic imaging techniques include those using radiation (plain radiography, fluoroscopy, angiography, and computed tomography).

Some diagnostic imaging does not involve radiation, such as magnetic resonance imaging (MRI) and ultrasound. More than half of these medical techniques were not possible twenty or twenty-five years ago.

The study and interpretation of these scans (imaging techniques) fall under the scientific discipline of radiology. Radiology is the study of human body images. Radiologists are physicians who have taken five or six years of additional training after medical school. Their additional studies taught them how to look at and understand medical imaging. Specialties include cardiovascular (study of the heart and blood vessels), thoracic (study of the chest), genitourinary (study of the kidneys, ureters, and bladder), gastrointestinal (study of

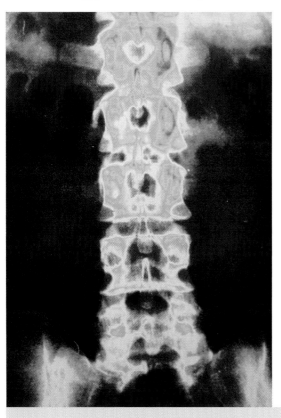

An X-ray image of the spine and pelvis

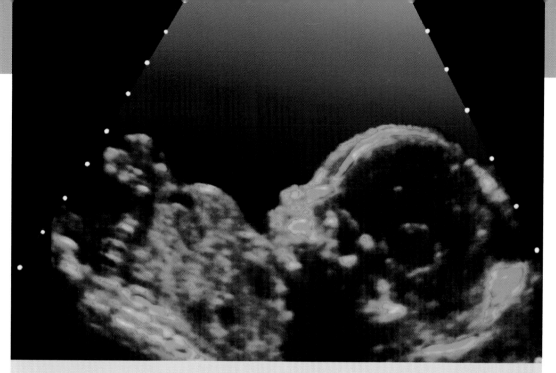

Doctors are able to monitor the progress of pregnant women and their fetuses using ultrasound images, such as the one above of a five-month-old fetus.

the stomach and intestines), musculoskeletal (study of the muscles and bones), neuroradiology (study of the brain and nerves), pediatric (study of children), and women's imaging (including obstetrics, gynecology, and mammography). Some radiologists specialize in radiation therapy (the treatment of diseases), but that is not the focus of this book.

Many of the recent advances in diagnostic imaging have the computer to thank. The computer receives and processes data. It also may manipulate data after processing it. For example, post-processing may involve the reconstruction of images in several layers. This allows doctors to see what kind of problem exists and where it is inside body tissue. Computers also give doctors a three-dimensional picture of body parts. Examples are CT scans and MRIs.

Each year new computers give more detail than old ones. Each new computer also takes images and develops film more quickly. Not long ago, children had to be sedated for CT scans. Today, the procedure goes so fast that children can be awake during the study. Among the benefits of the new imaging techniques are higher percentages of successful surgeries. Finding out problems earlier lets surgeons act faster.

There are also decreased rates of postsurgery complications. Surgeons can better see what they're doing, leading to less unnecessary surgery. Medical imaging pinpoints the problem, which lets surgeons make smaller incisions (cuts) to get into the body. This leaves less damage to tissues. For example, in the 1940s, there was a 90 percent risk of complications from brain surgery. Today the risk is only 2 percent. The difference lies in how much surgery has to be done.

A SHORT HISTORY OF THE X-RAY

The year is 1895. Wilhelm Konrad Roentgen, a German professor of physics, ponders scientific questions. In his laboratory, researchers using Crookes tubes (empty vacuum glass tubes through which an electric current passes) notice that nearby photographic plates have become foggy.

Roentgen later observed that when placed near a vacuum tube, a chemically coated plate glowed. He reasoned that the tube must be giving off some mysterious rays. In further experiments, he focused the electric current (or electrons) on a metal target. The mysterious rays bouncing off the metal target could now be focused on photographic film. Roentgen then made an X-ray picture of his wife's hand, showing her bones and wedding ring. He realized that the rays could pass through skin and muscle, but that bones absorbed or stopped the rays.

Because "x" is the scientific symbol for the unknown, Roentgen called the invisible rays X-rays. For many years, people called X-rays "Roentgen" rays. In medicine, the scientific

Wilhelm Konrad Roentgen (1845–1923) discovered X-rays through dramatic experiments and some accidents. For this, he was awarded the first Nobel Prize in physics for 1901. It was fifty years after Roentgen's discovery that neuroradiology became a new discipline.

study of X-rays is called roentgenology. The pictures produced are called roentgenograms. These days people still use the term X-ray to describe the film or the procedure, but the terms radiograph and radiographic film are more current terms.

Eventually the discovery of the X-ray revolutionized medical and surgical practice. X-rays provided useful information for scientific research of all kinds. In 1901, Roentgen's research of the X-ray earned him the first Nobel Prize in physics.

WHAT MAKES AN X-RAY?

If an electric current hits the negative terminal (the cathode) of a vacuum tube, making it glow white-hot, the tube gives off a stream of electrons called cathode rays. These rays move to the positive electrical terminal of the tube (the anode). Electrons striking the anode (the target) of the X-ray tube cause the atoms of the target to give off X-rays. Tungsten is the metal often used in targets because tungsten isn't easily melted by the heat that electrons produce. The higher the electronic voltage applied to the cathode rays, the shorter the X-rays given off.

X-RAY POWER

As part of the electromagnetic spectrum, X-rays are related to radio waves. X-rays have much shorter wavelengths, however.

These short wavelengths give X-rays their penetration power. X-rays can penetrate many substances that other rays cannot. The shorter the ray, the greater the penetration. Only gamma rays given off by radium and some other radioactive materials, and cosmic rays, are shorter than X-rays.

X-rays are also related to such waves as heat or infrared waves (as from an electric space heater or a kitchen range), visible light rays (as from your desk lamp), ultraviolet rays (as in a tanning parlor), and rays from cosmic radiation (as from stars, for example).

HOW MUCH IS TOO MUCH?

Too much radiation can be harmful. X-rays can burn or destroy tissue, alter chromosomal structure, and cause cancer. Reports give Clarence Madison Dally (1865–1904) the dubious distinction of being the first American to die from overexposure to X-rays. As a glassblower who worked in the laboratory of Thomas A. Edison, Dally used his hands to test the output of X-ray tubes. He died in spite of the amputation of both his arms.

People often wonder how much X-ray exposure is safe. To put things in perspective, everyone receives around 100 to 150 millirads each year from the environment—from the Sun, for example, or from radioactive substances, such as uranium, in the earth. A regular chest X-ray exposes a person to 10 to 20 millirads. Fluoroscopic studies, which we'll discuss later, expose people to much more radiation than a regular X-ray. For example, a barium study of the intestines exposes a person to about 1,200 millirads of X-ray.

How much radiation is safe? No one knows for sure. Therefore, doctors try to expose patients to the least amount of radiation possible. However, when a person's medical condition is serious, the benefits of X-ray diagnostic study may outweigh the potential risks. Hospitals, clinics, and radiology staff take precautions to minimize dangerous levels of radiation. They shield patients and staff with lead aprons. They also inspect equipment regularly.

PROPER USAGE AND TESTING PROCEDURES

Before ordering any kind of imaging study, the doctor (a radiologist or primary-care physician) must (1) take the patient's history (ask questions about the current problem and other past medical conditions) and (2) do a thorough examination of the patient. Only then can the physician decide which studies to order or whether any imaging studies are needed. In other words, for the physician (and ultimately for the patient) what *not* to order is as important as what *to* order.

For example, if you go to the doctor with an ache in your neck that you have had off and on for several months, the doctor will first take your history. After a further physical examination, he or she may suggest treatments such as massage or physical therapy exercises. The doctor may believe that imaging studies are not necessary at this time.

Imaging studies do not stand alone; they help in making a diagnosis. In ordering studies, the doctor has to consider such factors as the availability of equipment, the expertise of the personnel doing the studies, and the severity of the injury.

Modern imaging studies are not cheap. And although they are generally safe, they are not entirely risk-free. When deciding to use an imaging study, the physician hopes to find the location of the problem and its cause. When deciding which tests to use, doctors have to weigh the value of the possible result against the risks and costs of the study.

In addition to money, the word "cost" includes risks to the patient. These include the patient's worries about having the test, the possible inconvenience of going to a large medical center to have the test, and, in the case of young children, the possible necessity of sedation with *its* risks. During an MRI scan of the brain, for example, children under age five usually need to be given sedatives to keep them from moving around.

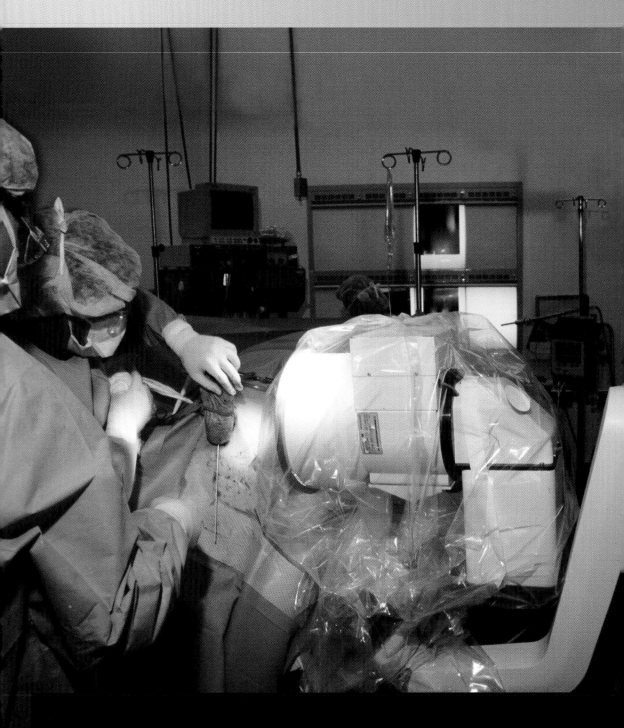

Surgeons using a portable fluoroscope X-ray system

2   Plain Radiography

Plain radiographs are also referred to as X-ray films or plain films. An X-ray beam passes through the patient and produces an image on film.

Try this: Sit on your bed and hold your hand under the rays of your bedside table lamp. Pretend that the light rays are X-rays, and the table is film. Now put a glass bottle beside your hand. The shadow your hand casts will be darker than the shadow from the glass because your hand is thicker (more dense) and the light does not go through your hand. The study of standard radiology is all about density.

The situation with X-rays is similar to the hand and glass scenario. When an X-ray machine takes a picture, X-rays reach the film and darken it. The more X-rays that reach the film, the darker that area will appear. If an object is dense, such as bone, it will absorb most of the X-rays and will appear white on the film. If the object is thin (not dense), its image will appear black because most of the X-ray beam reaches

Various body tissues absorb X-rays in differing amounts. For example, bone shows up white on X-ray film because it contains a great deal of calcium. Fluids, such as blood and soft tissue, look gray. Fat appears darker gray. Air appears almost black because it absorbs the least radiation.

Even in this era of sophisticated imaging techniques, plain radiographs account for more than 80 percent of all imaging studies. However, over the years, the means of receiving, reading, and interpreting the results have changed. In the early days, X-rays went through a part of the body such as the chest and onto a film inside a special cassette. (At one time, patients even had to hold their own cassettes!) After the film was developed, the doctor held the X-ray picture against a lighted screen to read it. Current technology includes computed radiography (CR) and direct radiography (DR), which can convert conventional X-rays to a digital format with a computerized laser scanner.

MAKING ADJUSTMENTS

The X-ray technologist can adjust the machine to increase the intensity of the X-ray beam. For example, a chest radiograph in a heavy person will need a stronger beam than an X-ray of a thin person's chest. There are also times when multiple radiographs must be made of the same area.

For example, someone runs into you at hockey practice, and you land on your right elbow on the ice. You're taken to the hospital for X-rays of the elbow. You sit there for a couple of hours, and your elbow hurts. You thought you were finished with this picture-taking session, but the technologist asks you to go back to the waiting room.

Fractures of the elbow are often difficult to see. Two or three films may be necessary to get it right. After reading anterior-posterior views (views from above and below) and lateral views (views at right angles to each other), the radiologist or technologist can judge whether more views are necessary. Oblique (angled) projections may help to confirm questionable findings. Sometimes the radiologist asks the technologist to take films of the other (normal) elbow for comparison.

After viewing preliminary results, the technologist, radiologist, or both may decide they need more images.

CONTRAST MEDIA

Contrast agents allow technicians to see parts of the body that cannot otherwise be seen using X-rays. These include soft tissue organs such as the kidneys or intestines. The use of contrast agents began in the early 1900s. Substances are swallowed, injected, or given as enemas. The denseness of barium sulfate or iodine-containing materials allow them to absorb the X-ray beam. The outline of barium, for example, may show the cavity of the stomach or the inside of the intestinal tract. Because it is safe, air is sometimes used as a contrast agent. For a baby, an air-contrast enema may be used to study a suspected intestinal obstruction.

When contrast agents are swallowed or given as enemas, there is little risk to the patient. If they are given intravenously, there is a bit more risk. About 5 percent of patients have a mild reaction to the contrast agent. These reactions may include a metallic taste, a warm feeling under their skin, nausea, vomiting, or wheezing.

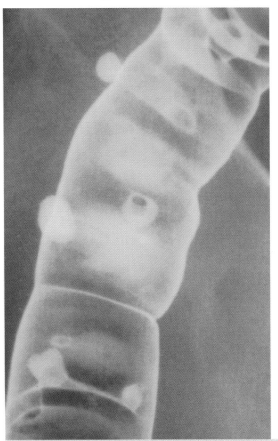

This X-ray image of a colon affected by diverticulosis was taken using barium as the contrast agent.

How Could We Know?

An interesting (and potentially dangerous) marketing idea, which began in the 1920s, put floor-model fluoroscopes in shoe stores. Customers who put their feet into the machine could see their bones. The radiation exposure might be several minutes; the exposure of a regular X-ray film today is more like a fraction of one second. Because of the radiation dangers, the shoe-store machines were discontinued in the 1950s.

About 1 in every 1,000 patients has more severe side effects, such as an allergic reaction.

FLUOROSCOPY

X-rays are able to affect certain chemicals and make them fluoresce (glow). These chemicals will continue to glow as long as the X-rays are hitting them. Fluoroscopy imaging uses this technique. Originally, fluoroscopy substituted a screen of light-emitting crystals for the photographic plate. The fluoroscopy screen is much like a TV screen.

Currently, fluoroscopy is used to capture live images of a body part. After an X-ray beam is transmitted through the patient, the X-rays strike a fluorescent plate. Fluoroscopic light is faint unless it is electronically amplified. Today's fluoroscopic rooms have image intensification machines. These machines make the images much easier to see, even in a lighted room.

With fluoroscopy, doctors can watch bodily functions in action on a TV screen. For example, they can see a needle being used to draw out a collection of pus from a body cavity. In a cardiac catheterization, the fluoroscope helps keep track of the movement of a small tube through the body's circulatory system.

At the time of the live action, the technologist can also take individual static radiographs. Sometimes the action is so rapid, as in swallowing, it is helpful to use cineradiography. Cineradiography records successive fluoroscopic images on videotape. It is like a "swallowing movie" that you can fast-forward, slow down, or replay.

ANGIOGRAPHY

Angiography is the study of blood vessels using an injected contrast medium. The contrast agent (sometimes called dye) is radiopaque; it absorbs X-rays and helps show small vascular details such as obstructions and narrowing.

Angiography uses X-rays to produce an angiogram (picture). The procedure is invasive. It requires the insertion

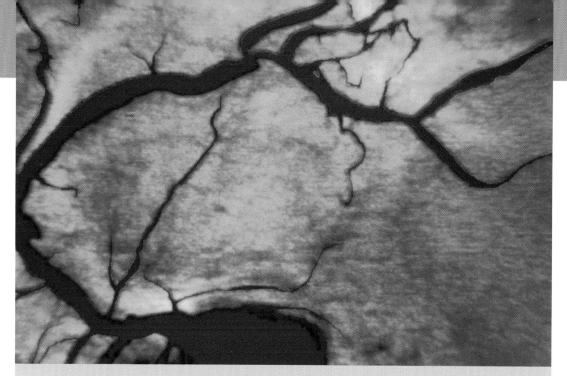

This angiogram shows coronary artherosclerois in a patient. Because of the invasive nature of angiography, 3-D coronary magnetic resonance angiography (MRA) is becoming a safer, noninvasive alternative.

of a small, specially shaped catheter (tube) into the patient's artery or vein. The radiopaque material absorbs the X-rays and casts a shadow of the injected vessels onto the X-ray film or fluoroscope. An example of angiography is testing for cardiac disease: an injection is made into the heart to view the coronary arteries and vessels coming from it.

Currently, many angiograms are done by noninvasive means. The MRI scanner can be set to show flowing blood without the need for a catheter injection. Doctors can visualize large arteries or veins with this technique.

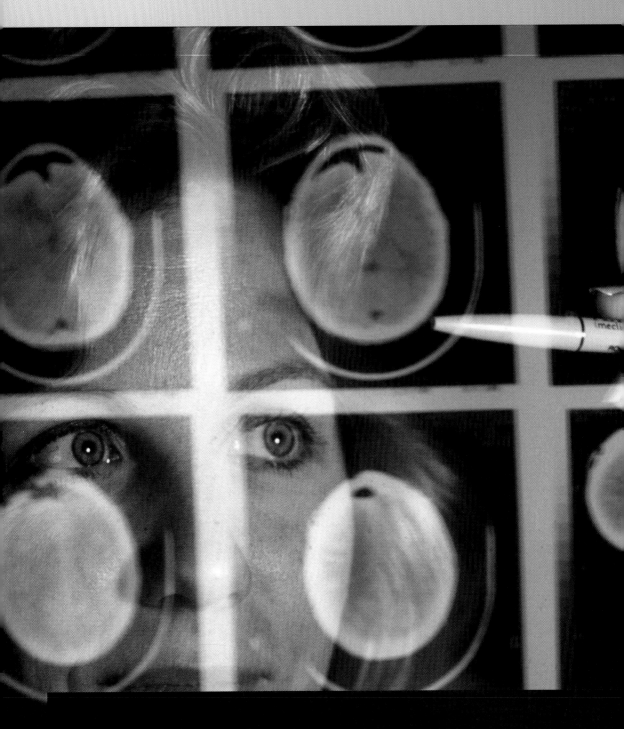

A medical technician reads a CT scan

3 ⟩ Tomography

When you hear the term "CAT scan," does your mind picture a large calico? Maybe not. What if you get a head injury while playing soccer? Will you need a CAT scan? Not necessarily.

CAT scans (computerized axial tomography) or CT scans (computerized tomography) are similar terms for the same procedure. Today doctors most often use the term "CT scan."

Before looking into the mechanisms of CT scans, we need to define the word "tomography," which means "thin slice" or "thin section." To help understand the concept of tomography, imagine your body sawed into slices like a loaf of bread. Of course, doctors wouldn't do this, even though it would help them see inside your body much better than most other procedures. That's why the CT scan is so special. Its slices are pictures of small layers of your body. When all these picture slices are put together, a computer collects them and shows a complete image of the body or body part on a video screen.

CT SCAN TECHNOLOGY

Most scientific discoveries result from the efforts of many people. Scientists often work together and/or build on each others' work. Sometimes scientists in different parts of the world make the same discovery at the same time.

Such was the case with tomography. Several medical imaging inventors came up with the idea of a machine that would get a clear image of the plane of interest (a slice) with the area around it purposely blurred. Equipment manufacturers, however, considered the concept impractical.

Finally, in 1937 in St. Louis, a machine was built that moved the X-ray tube and film while the focal planes did not move. The machine captured a clear image of a single slice. The focus moved from that plane to the next. For more than thirty years, plain tomography gave doctors their best chance of seeing hidden organs. Each tomograph has one focus: the pictures in that plane only. This makes it more useful for diagnostic purposes than ordinary films.

COMPUTERIZED AXIAL TOMOGRAPHY

Computed (or computerized) tomography, which uses principles of radiology coupled with computer technology, came into usage in the 1970s. Although many people worked on this concept, Godfrey Hounsfield of Great Britain gets much of the credit for turning theory into practice.

Computerized tomography was invented because a need for better visualization of the brain and other organs existed. Computerized tomography improves on conventional tomography because it is much faster. Hounsfield used gamma rays (and later, X-rays) with a detector on a rotating frame. He added a digital computer to make detailed cross-sectional images. By today's standards, Hounsfield's equipment seems primitive, but he received a Nobel Prize in 1979 for his discovery.

We can use many different types of comparisons to explain how a CT scan is done. Remember the earlier experiment with your hand under the bedside lamp? Now imagine the lamp and the bedside table spinning around your hand.

But this is still far from what happens, especially if you need a CT scan for a head injury. In this case, you will most likely lie on your back on a stretcher. Your head will be moved into the gantry, the huge housing for all of the scanning equipment, such as the X-ray tube, detector array, and high-voltage generator. It's like putting your head in the hole of a very large doughnut. The table moves in and out of an open circular tunnel, taking images of your head.

As you lie still, the machine will take X-rays from the front of your head to the back. Taking continuous pictures, the machine moves constantly around your head. Special electronic detectors—100 times more sensitive than ordinary X-ray film—align directly opposite the X-ray tube. The detectors convert the exiting beam into electrical impulses depending on how much X-ray the intervening tissue absorbs.

The computer records each electrical impulse generated and calculates the X-ray absorption, or density, of any given spot or cube, called a voxel, of tissues. The intersection of the beam coming from many angles determines the density of the voxel at the place where the beams intersect. The absorption value of the voxel is expressed in Hounsfield units. The computer then prints out the density of each voxel on a single film of that cross-sectional, or axial, unit.

Next the stretcher will move your head five millimeters farther into the machine and take another picture. In this way, the machine obtains several (ten to twenty) cross-sectional views of your head and brain.

NEW STANDARDS IN CT SCANS

New machines can take each image in a second or less. In other words, each second a five-millimeter slice is filmed. The machine will take a total of twenty to twenty-five contiguous pictures (slices next to each other). To do this, the machine rotates twenty to twenty-five times. In a CT scan of the abdomen, the slices are often ten millimeters thick.

Radiologists talk about slices because, in fact, CT scans present their data as a series of slices. It is much like pulling apart a loaf of bread and examining each slice. What the doctor really sees is the front face of the slice, not the thickness, because when the picture is made, it is a two-dimensional representation.

Most of the time, doctors get all of the information they need from a "plain" (no contrast used) CT scan. For example, if a pediatrician suspects that a newborn baby has bleeding inside the brain (an intracranial hemorrhage), a plain CT scan—where blood shows up clearly—may help figure out exactly where in the brain the bleeding is and how serious it is. Contrast enhancement, on the other hand, might help to identify a tumor and/or the tiny blood vessels in the tumor.

If a contrast agent is needed, it is injected and the whole procedure is repeated. However, radiologists often know ahead of time when they will have to do a contrast-enhanced scan. An example of this would be an adult or child suspected of having a brain tumor. If contrast agents are used, they are usually the same agents used in other imaging studies and have the same risks.

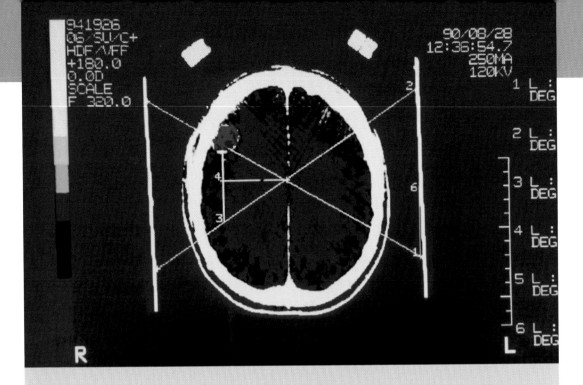

This CT scan of the brain shows the regions where a tumor is growing in red.

From the axial slices, a computer can calculate and print out images that are sagittal (like slicing the bread lengthwise from side-to-side) or coronal (like slicing a cake to make layers). Occasionally, such as in plastic surgery of the face, a doctor might need a three-dimensional rendering (picture). A three-dimensional rendering is more difficult to obtain because many thin slices are required to calculate all of the tiny curves and angles of the facial bone, for example. The procedure is also more difficult for the computer because it has to make a model in three dimensions with a great deal of data to process.

The images can be displayed on a TV monitor or be saved on a disk or videotape for later use. With present-day digital technology, the doctor can view the stored images on a TV screen in the office or at home. Because the images often contain a large amount of data, a special transmission line is necessary. To protect patient privacy, the network must be secured.

One of the exciting things about CT studies is that they show a large number of body structures at the same time. For example, if you have a chronic pain in your midsection, a CT scan could show your liver, kidneys, pancreas, spleen, aorta, and other structures all at once. CT scans are very sensitive; they reveal up to 96 percent of lesions (diseased or injured tissue). And, although the machine takes many pictures during the scan, the total amount of radiation may be less than the radiation from a plain X-ray. However, the image may lack specificity. Tumors, infection sites, and strokes sometimes look alike on the scan. Another imaging study, such as the more expensive MRI scan, may be necessary. One drawback is that the machine itself makes some people feel claustrophobic. In such cases, patients may need to take a mild sedative to help them relax during the scan.

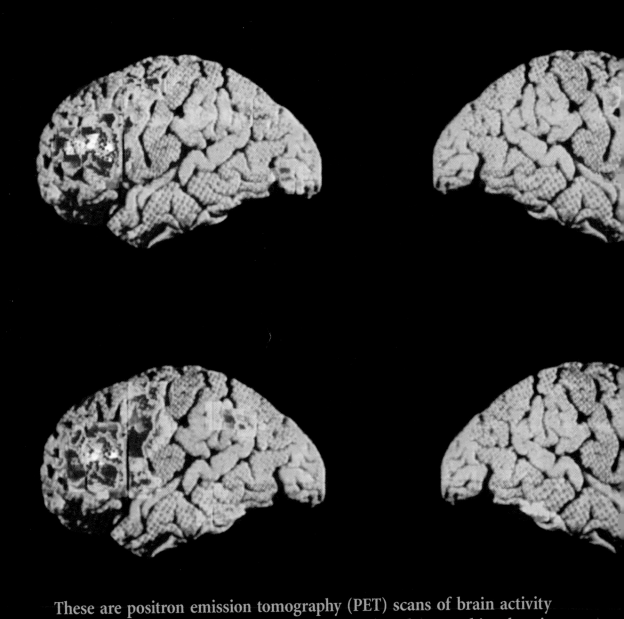

These are positron emission tomography (PET) scans of brain activity *(colored regions)* in a normal person *(above)* and in a schizophrenic patient *(below)* that were taken while the patients were speaking. The scans show heightened activity in the schizophrenic brain.

4 Nuclear Medicine

Nuclear medicine is the branch of medicine that uses radioactive isotopes to diagnose and treat diseases. Also called nuclear imaging, radionuclide imaging, or scintigraphy, nuclear medicine imaging is based on the discovery that the nuclei of radioactive elements or compounds (nuclides) contain excess energy and are thus unstable. To reach a more stable state, the nucleus emits excess energy in the form of radiation. The three types of radiation include alpha and beta particles (small bits of energy from the nucleus) and gamma rays (which are much like X-rays).

Although radioactive elements occur naturally, they can also be produced artificially. Radionuclides used in nuclear medicine are artificially made. They are used as tracers for finding out information about the structure, function, and size of organs and tissue.

In nuclear medicine, doctors usually give the patient intravenous radioactive material (a radionu-clide). These radioactive materials are not dangerous because they have a short radioactive life, or half-life; their radioactivity lasts only a short time. The most frequently used radionuclides, such as technetium-99m, decay quickly and have half-lives of only hours. Most of these materials cannot be detected in the body twenty-four hours after administration.

Radionuclides are attached to certain radioactive carrier compounds. Their radioactivity concentrates in diseased tissue. This includes abcesses or tumors in various body parts, such as the thyroid gland, the heart, the lungs, or bone.

If you need a nuclear scan of a bone, you will go to a nuclear medicine unit and be injected with a radioactive substance in one of your veins. After a wait, you'll lie on a table or stretcher under a gamma camera or another radionuclide detector. A computer will translate signals from the scanner into images that will be recorded onto X-ray film, camera film, or a TV monitor.

To do bone scans in nuclear medicine, doctors use a diphosphonate-technetium combination. This combination is a bone-seeking radiopharmaceutical. After attaching to the bone, these radioactive chemicals gradually leave the body through urination. Fifty to sixty percent of the radiopharmaceutical localizes in the bone in three to four hours. Half of the radiation will be gone in twenty-four hours. Doctors may make a diagnosis on the basis of a

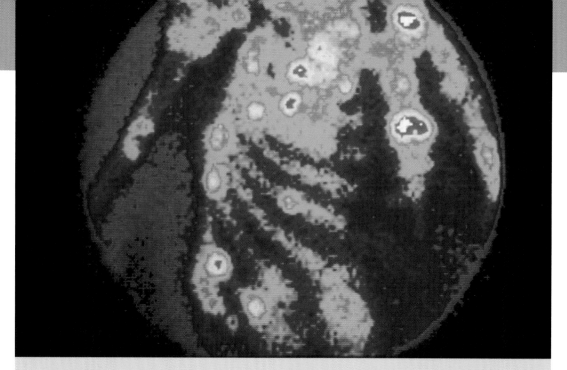

Technetium bone scans are a type of nuclear imaging specifically used for diagnosing diseases in bone matter. This scan shows metastatic bone cancer.

specific tissue's absorption of the radioactive isotope. Bone absorbs technetium. In other types of scans, the thyroid absorbs radioactive iodine, and white cells absorb radioactive gallium.

The radiologist reading the scan will look for "hot areas," or areas of excessive radioactivity. A hot area may be normal, as in the growing part at the end of a bone (the diaphasis), or it may be abnormal, as at the site of a bone infection (osteomyelitis). A "cold area" (lack of radioactivity) might occur, for example, in an area of a bone cyst; this cold area would also be abnormal.

POSITRON EMISSION TOMOGRAPHY

Positron emission tomography combines nuclear scanning with biochemical analysis. PET is a nuclear medicine technique that produces an image of tissue or organ functioning. However, the image looks more like a silhouette than a three-dimensional picture. The word "positron" refers to the particles (positrons) that the scanner records. "Emission" refers to the fact that the site being imaged emits radioactivity. "Tomography" refers to the images made of body planes as part of the study.

Unlike PET, most other imaging techniques show

A radiologist examines a series of PET scans. PET scans can detect a site of accelerated metabolic activity, such as a malformation or a tumor, which is not detected by anatomic scanning devices, such as CT scans or MRI scans.

only the anatomy of body organs. PET scanning reveals the physiological or metabolic activities going on inside these organs. For example, PET can show blood flow in various parts of the body or images of glucose metabolism. Such information tells doctors if an organ is working properly. If the organ is not functioning, the PET may show the location where the problem exists. PET is a diagnostic tool that helps doctors react quickly to a possibly serious problem in a patient. PET scanning became available for medical (largely research) purposes in the 1980s.

THE PET SCAN IN ACTION

Like other medical imaging, PET scans work by bombarding a body part with image-generating media. In this case, radio-isotopes are used. Radioisotopes emit positrons (positively charged particles with almost no mass). When a positron strikes an electron, two gamma rays (photons) are emitted at right angles to the collision. From the information gathered, the computer makes cross-sectional images of the organ.

In a patient with epilepsy, for example, a PET scan can identify the site in the brain of the seizure discharge. The PET scan shows a rapidly metabolizing glucose at the time of the seizure. On the other hand, when that same site is between seizures, the metabolism will be less than normal or will appear as a cold area on the image.

ADVANTAGES AND DISADVANTAGES

The isotopes used in PET scans have very short half-lives. A cyclotron produces them by bombarding elements with high-speed neutrons. They must be used immediately (in minutes to hours). Technologists have to do the scans quickly, before the radioactivity is gone.

PET scans often use the isotope fluorine-18, which is incorporated into deoxyglucose to allow the measurement of brain glucose metabolism, as in the epilepsy example. Doctors may use a PET scan to measure the extent of muscle damage after a heart attack. A PET scan of the whole body is sometimes done to detect widespread metastatic cancer.

Disadvantages include the high cost and the necessity of having a cyclotron and sophisticated computer equipment. Also needed are highly trained professionals to read images that are somewhat blurry.

SPECT (SINGLE PHOTON EMISSION COMPUTED TOMOGRAPHY)

SPECT first came into use in the late 1960s but was not widely available until the 1980s. SPECT (single photon emission computed tomography) evolved from SPET (single photon emission tomography), which did not use computers. It is similar to CT but uses a special lens called a collimator.

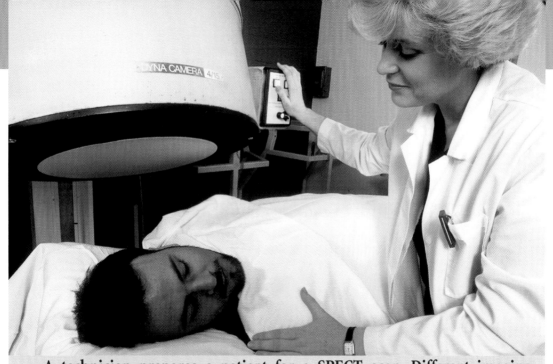

A technician prepares a patient for a SPECT scan. Different imaging methods on the same site may show different things. For example, a seizure source in the brain may show decreased metabolism (PET), decreased blood flow (SPECT), and structural abnormalities (MRI/CT scans).

In some ways, SPECT is similar to PET, though SPECT radioisotopes decay by emitting a *single* gamma ray, and their half-lives are much longer than those used in PET scans. Like the PET, the image produced is not sharp. But, like other radioactive scanning techniques, hot areas (tumors) or cold areas (brain cysts or scarring) may be important diagnostic signals. While PET looks at metabolic processes, SPECT looks mainly at the blood flow to an area. Fortunately, the two processes often complement each other. For example, in a patient with epilepsy, doctors may consider surgery at an active seizure site in the brain. The more the imaging tests are in agreement, the more likely that surgery will be accurate and successful.

ADVANTAGES AND DISADVANTAGES

The properties of the radioactivity used in a SPECT scan offer advantages and disadvantages. One advantage is that there is more time to study the blood flow to an area. This includes additional time to study the uptake of a radionuclide in a certain tissue, which is directly related to the blood flow to that area. For example, a technetium radionuclide will flow rapidly to a metabolically active brain lesion. The fat-soluble portion of this compound will be metabolized slowly, providing several hours for the reading. Another advantage is convenience: A cyclotron is not needed to make the radionuclide, which makes SPECT less expensive than PET.

A disadvantage is that SPECT exposes the body to low doses of radioactivity for up to several days. The intestines and kidneys have to excrete the radioactivity, exposing them to radioactivity over a longer period of time than normal.

MRI (MAGNETIC RESONANCE IMAGING)

The development of MRI technology has had many contributors. Among them was Dr. Raymond Damadian and his colleagues at Downstate Medical Center in Brooklyn, New York. These doctors worked for seven years to produce a machine they called "Indomitable." In 1977, Indomitable was the first

MRI scanner to be used with a person. Despite the skeptics, MRI technology was being widely used by the mid-1980s.

To understand MRI technology, we need to know something about magnets, atoms, radio frequency, imaging techniques, and computers. We also need to know how MRI helps to visualize hydrogen ions (protons) in the body to produce images. The magnet is the largest part of the MRI system. Its role is to align the hydrogen nuclei. The main magnet creates a stable and intense magnetic field around the patient's head or body. Other magnets in the machine, such as gradient magnets, can change the magnetic field and create varying hydrogen orbits.

Billions of atoms make up the human body, and each atom has a nucleus. Manipulation of the nucleus helped scientists uncover the potential of MRI. Although the body contains all kinds of atoms, MRI is "hydrogen imaging." Because the human body is 98 percent water (H_2O), it provides the possibility for imaging almost every living tissue. MRI images protons, which are the same as hydrogen ions.

Hydrogen ions naturally spin on an axis. If placed in a magnetic field, the axis can be changed; the ions line up. Unlike X-rays, which read density, MRI surveys the location of hydrogen ions to create an image of tissue structure. An MRI gives an exact picture of tissue, organs, and detectable defects.

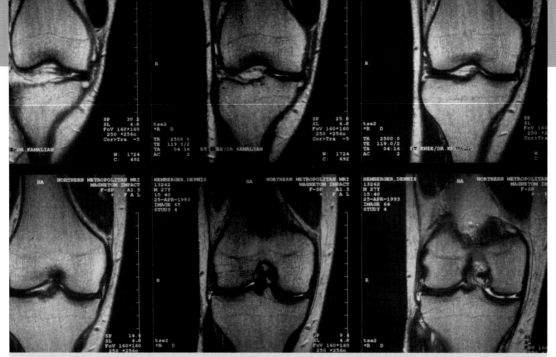

An MRI of a knee. Unlike other imaging techniques, an MRI does not expose the body to radiation. An MRI can make the bone/soft tissue borders more distinct.

Radio waves can affect objects differently. MRI technology uses radio frequency pulses to direct the spinning orbits of hydrogen ions. Changing these orbits gives off energy, another radio frequency pulse, which can be measured and converted into pictures. The returning radio waves come directly from the tissue. The best part about MRI technology is that radio waves are not ionizing radiation, and therefore they are safe.

IMAGING TECHNIQUES

The MRI machine is set to yield two major sequences. A T1 (Time one) sequence gives a superior image of anatomy structure. T1 is the sequence used when contrast agents are injected. The T2 sequence shows water more effectively and is superior in identifying abnormalities, such as edema (water in the tissues) due to a stroke or tumor. (As early as 1971, Dr. Raymond Damadian and his team had shown with these readings that cancerous tissue differed from healthy tissue.)

The MRI can even show problems with the insulation on nerve tissue (demyelination), as in multiple sclerosis. Another recent technique, diffusion-weighted MRI, is even more sensitive than the T2 for recognizing edema from an early stroke. As with CT scans, the picture can be printed on film or used with digital imaging on a TV screen.

THE COMPUTER

Transfer of some of the complicated algorithms used in CT scanning helped lead to the development of the MRI. Medical technology has also borrowed from other fields, such as mining, seismology, and cartoon animation. The computer is the best machine for these complicated jobs because it is able to process data very quickly. Computers make MRI technology possible by translating radio-wave signals into detailed cross-sectional images.

THE MRI PROCEDURE

The MRI unit contains the massive main magnet, which is always on. The unit structure is approximately six or seven feet high and equally wide. As a patient, you will lie on your back on a special table that slides into the magnet through a two-foot-wide tunnel in the middle of the machine. Whether you go in head or feet first depends on the tissue being imaged.

Be prepared for a loud knocking noise; this is not a silent machine. The loud knocking noise is caused by the gradients (small magnets) expanding against the supporting brackets. The MRI scanner will be able to pick out voxels (three-dimensional cubes) maybe only one millimeter on each side. It will make a two-dimensional or three-dimensional map of the tissue type. The computer will integrate this information and create two-dimensional images (the usual) or three-dimensional models. The whole procedure takes from thirty to sixty minutes.

ADVANTAGES AND DISADVANTAGES OF MRI

Some advantages of MRI over other imaging techniques are:

◆ Lack of radiation makes it safe for children and for repeated scanning of the same person.

- The level of detail produced exceeds the detail of other imaging techniques.

- MRI has the ability to image in any plane (axial, coronal, and sagittal) without repositioning the patient.

- In an MRI, bones are clearly defined at the interface of the bone and surrounding tissue. For example, in the posterior part of the skull there is a lot of lumpy bone, and in the face the bones have many nooks and crannies. CT scans may show a fuzziness where bone and tissue meet. MRI produces a sharper image.

- MRI can image most body tissues; it can show such structures as blood vessels and nerves.

MRI has some disadvantages, too:

- Magnetic strength can be a dangerous thing. Stories abound about the magnets' power to pull metal objects (such as paper clips, keys, scissors, stethoscopes, IV poles, and even oxygen tanks) toward the patient and into the machine. Even worse, accidents have occurred with metal *inside* a patient. After an MRI, a metal worker went blind because the magnet moved microscopic metal particles in his eyes, damaging their surrounding structures. A survivor of an aneurysm died during an MRI because the magnet tore off the metal clips holding together a blood vessel in her brain, causing her to bleed to death.

- The patient must stay absolutely motionless during the procedure. (Minor motion does not have as much impact on a CT scan.) Therefore, a sedative is often necessary for a child having an MRI scan.

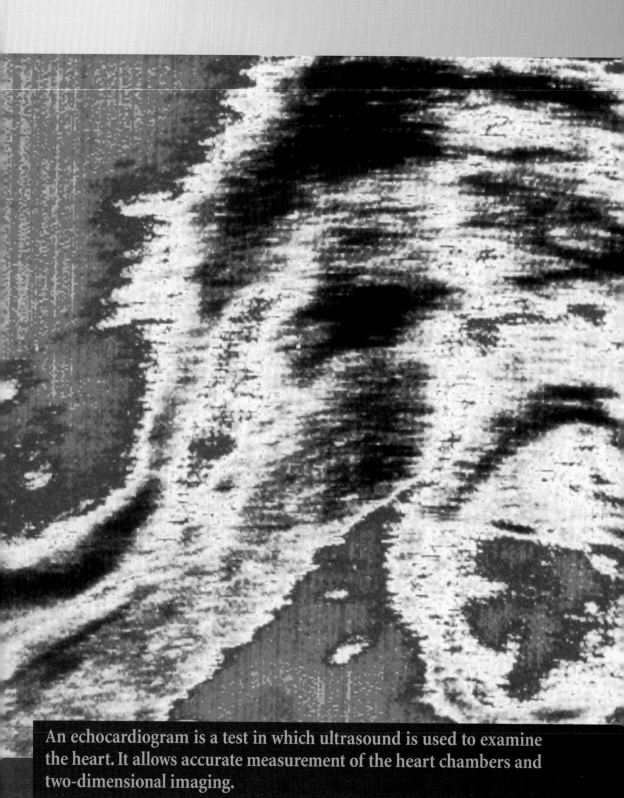

An echocardiogram is a test in which ultrasound is used to examine the heart. It allows accurate measurement of the heart chambers and two-dimensional imaging.

5 Ultrasound

Ultrasound (ultrasonography) is an imaging technique that uses sound waves and their echoes. Whales, dolphins, and bats also use sound to "see." With ultrasound, electronic sound waves are sent out. When these waves hit an object, they bounce back. The returning sound waves form a pattern of the object they have hit. Computers translate these patterns into an image on a video screen. Scientists used ultrasound to locate the hulk of the sunken *Titanic*.

Ultrasound is high-frequency sound (over 20,000 cycles per second). Piezoelectric quartz or ceramic crystal is the most important part on the ultrasound transducer probe. Pierre and Jacques Curie discovered the piezoelectric (pressure electric) effect in 1880.

The transducer converts an electric signal into sound waves. Placed anywhere on the body, ultrasonic energy can then be transmitted through body tissues. Sound wave echoes bounce back from the tissue of interest. The reflected sound is converted back into an electric signal and recorded on film.

The transducer's piezoelectric crystals can transform electricity into sound waves and vice versa. Therefore, the transducer becomes both the sender and the receiver. For example, a technologist might place the transducer probe on a patient's abdominal wall, move it from side to side, and possibly discover an enlarged kidney or a kidney tumor. The transducer uses echoes to visualize internal organs, vessels, and cavities. An injured spleen might reveal a collection of blood. Specialized probes inserted into body openings can study organs from the inside. For example, a probe in the esophagus can study the nearby heart, a probe in the vagina can study the uterus, and a probe in the rectum can study the prostate. As the study progresses, medical professionals, and sometimes even the patient, can see the imaged tissue on the monitor. The machine can also print out the images.

HUMAN CONTROLLED IMAGING

Ultrasound technologists are key to the outcome of the study. They have to decide which frequency pulses to send, how to aim the transducer probe, and when to make a film or a photograph. Each of these is a critical decision.

Most ultrasound studies produce two-dimensional pictures. However, sophisticated computer programs can make three-dimensional representations. For example, in fetal

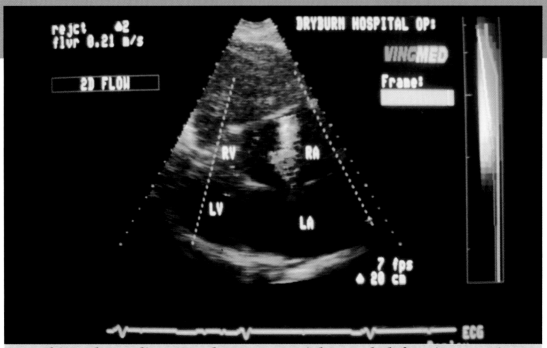

This echocardiogram shows an atrial septal defect in a patient. Echocardiograms are capable of displaying a cross-sectional slice of the beating heart, including the chambers, valves, and the major blood vessels that exit from the left and right ventricles.

ultrasound, doctors use specialized software to visualize the unborn baby in the uterus. They can detect malformations in the heart or the spine.

ECHOCARDIOGRAPHY

There are three types of heart ultrasonography (echocardiography). The first is regular two-dimensional, cross-sectional ultrasound views using a probe on the chest wall. The second is the M (movement) mode, which pictures the movement of heart muscles and can also show heart wall thickness and chamber size. Doctors use this procedure to estimate cardiac functioning. The third is Doppler ultrasound, which determines the velocity of moving objects. In ultrasound, the transducer sends a sound wave that bounces off the red cells flowing in a blood vessel and comes back to the transducer. As the red cells get closer to the transducer, this bouncing comes back more frequently, producing a higher-pitched sound. These differences help calculate the speed of blood flow.

Doppler ultrasound can measure the flow of blood (cardiac output) as well as pressure gradients between the heart's chambers. Doppler ultrasound is used all over the body to evaluate blood flow or obstruction of flow in the carotid artery in the neck that goes to the brain, or in an artery or vein in the leg.

ADVANTAGES AND DISADVANTAGES

One big advantage of ultrasound is its portability. An ultrasound machine is small enough to fit on a wheeled cart. Doctors can order ultrasound images of the brain that can be done at the patient's bedside. A very sick infant can avoid the risks of a trip to the CT or MRI machine. The transducer probe applied to an infant's anterior fontanel (a baby's "soft spot") at the top of the head can yield coronal and sagittal views. Using this technology, doctors can diagnose cysts, malformations, hydrocephalus (an accumulation of fluid in the brain), blood clots, hemorrhages, and strokes. Ultrasound creates real-time movies of flowing blood, bowel contractions, and the beating heart without the use of radiation or invasive techniques. Another advantage of ultrasound is its cost—ultrasound is much less expensive than either CT or MRI.

Ultrasound has a few disadvantages. One is the fuzziness of the picture. More important than in other imaging techniques, excellence of interpretation depends on the experience of the radiologist. The outcome of the study is also technologist dependent. And, in the case of gastrointestinal ultrasound, there is the problem of unwanted echoes from gas in the stomach and intestines.

The M2A Capsule Endoscope is a new tool used to examine the gastrointestinal tract. The system uses a disposable miniature video camera contained in a disposable capsule that is ingested by a patient and delivers high-quality color images in a painless and noninvasive manner.

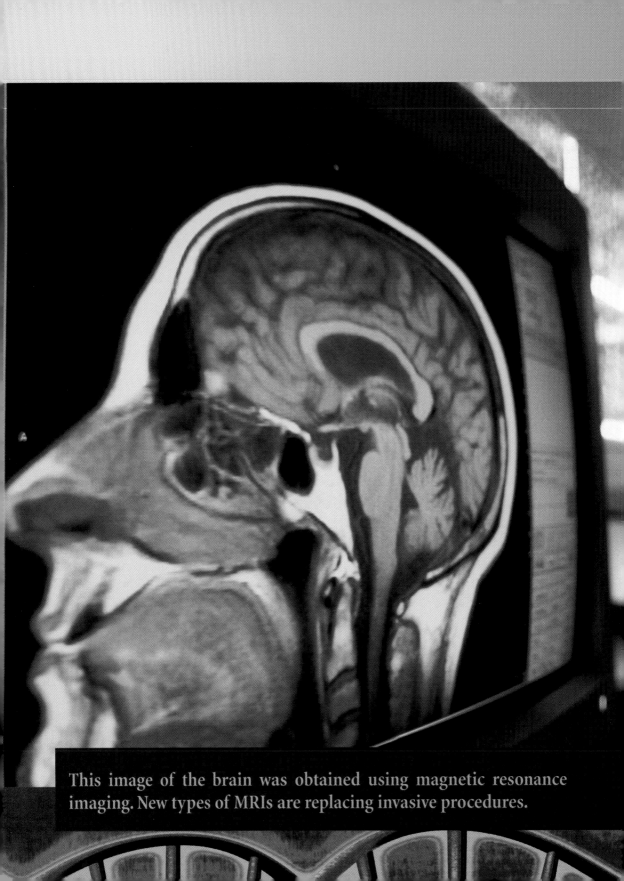

This image of the brain was obtained using magnetic resonance imaging. New types of MRIs are replacing invasive procedures.

6

The Future of Medical Imaging

The future of medical imaging promises nearly unlimited possibilities. Many experts believe that medical imaging is the most exciting field of science today. Some of the newer technologies such as magnetic resonance spectroscopy (MRS) and functional magnetic resonance imaging (fMRI) are moving from research settings to clinical applications.

MRS (MAGNETIC RESONANCE SPECTROSCOPY)

One type of MRS study examines *structure*. For example, we could ask this question: At a site of interest in the brain, are there more nerve cells (neuronal tissue) or supporting cells (glial tissue)? We might compare the nerve cells to an office computer and the supporting cells to the walls and floor of the office. N-acetyl aspartate (NAA) is a chemical marker for nerve cells ("the computer"). Choline and creatine are chemical markers for the surface membrane of glial cells ("the walls and floor").

Ratios (for example, NAA/choline) would show a high value (the NAA peak would be high on the spectrograph while the choline would be low) in an area of many nerve cells. The same ratio would have a low value in an area of much supporting tissue (glial cells). In an area of scarring or in an area with few nerve cells, the peak of NAA would be low on the spectrograph (a graph with a series of peaks, one for each compound), while the one for choline would be high. These two examples show the use of spectroscopy to describe the structural components of an area of the brain. In other words, is the tested area structurally rich in nerve cells or in supportive tissue?

In another application of MRS, researchers and physicians can assess *metabolic* function in the same area of the brain, and in the same voxel. A high-energy phosphate compound (let's say phosphocreatine—PCr) reflects a metabolically active area; for example, an area of normal nerve cells in the brain stem. Inorganic phosphate (Pi) is low in this metabolically active area. Therefore, a ratio—PCr/Pi would have a high value in a metabolically active area.

Often in these studies, doctors compare a possibly damaged area to an undamaged area. They compare one part of the brain (for example, the frontal gyrus) to the same area on the other side of the brain to show the extent of damage on one side. A plaque of damaged tissue (from multiple sclerosis, for example) could be compared to a nearby area of normal tissue.

FMRI (FUNCTIONAL OR FAST MAGNETIC RESONANCE IMAGING)

In addition to regular MRI with its ability to image vital organs, such as the brain and heart, scientists have started using "fast" or "functional" MRI, which has the ability to evaluate function.

Functional imaging goes beyond passive visualization. It shows living tissues in action. For example, fMRI can detect and follow (as the person changes tasks) areas of the brain used in reading. It can show places in the brain in which a normal reader's brain differs from that of a patient with dyslexia.

How can fMRI do this? By taking rapid pictures (30 to 100 frames per second), fMRI can distinguish between oxygenated and deoxygenated blood; the latter is paramagnetic (very active). Deoxygenated blood magnetizes, or activates, protons (hydrogen ions) as much as 100,000 times more than when the blood is full of oxygen. There is a dramatic difference between the oxygen-filled blood that supplies a metabolically active area of the brain (for example, a site of reading activity) and the deoxygenated blood leaving that area. The metabolically active area of a "normal reader" lights up. Seiji Ogawa, an fMRI pioneer, called this effect BOLD (blood oxygen level dependent) contrast imaging. The test goes very fast, so the doctor can ask the patient to repeat the task or to modify the task slightly to confirm or change results.

WHAT'S NEXT?

For each imaging technique discussed, looking toward the future is the next step to creating new technology. For example, improvements in MRI may make complete body scans possible in a matter of minutes. MRI may also provide real-time images to guide internal surgery while patient and doctor are in the operating room. Magnet design may improve enough to eliminate the claustrophobia caused by being placed inside the machine. In ultrasound, the machine will have more memory, will get smaller, and will become more portable. The transducer probe will also shrink and become easier to insert and focus.

TELERADIOLOGY/INFORMATICS

Another revolution in the medical imaging of the future will involve extensive developments in telecommunications networking. The picture archive and communications system (PACS) allows images to be stored in digital format for wide distribution. For example, to speed up medical decision making, an emergency room will have the ability to transmit images locally (within a hospital) and on other wide-area networks.

Although the future is difficult to predict, more sophisticated imaging and image-guided procedures will almost certainly make possible quicker, more accurate, and less invasive diagnosis of diseases.

Glossary

algorithm A step-by-step procedure to solve a problem by a computer, using specific mathematical or logical operations.

aneurysm A bubbling of the wall of an artery or a vein.

angiography Also called arteriography or venography. Radiography after the injection of contrast material.

catheter A tube that allows fluids to pass through it.

cathode The negative electrode of devices such as electron tubes and X-ray tubes; the electrode towards which positively charged ions move.

cyclotron A machine that accelerates charged particles to high energies, often making them radioactive.

Doppler ultrasound A diagnostic instrument that emits an ultrasonic beam into the body.

echocardiography The use of ultrasound to inspect the heart and the large blood vessels.

electromagnetic Involving both electricity and magnetism.

electron A negatively charged particle smaller than an atom that orbits the positive nucleus.

fluoroscopy An X-ray technique in which the image is shown on a television monitor as it is being created.

gamma camera Also called gamma scintillation camera. A camera used in nuclear scans to measure how much radioactivity is being absorbed by an organ or tissue.

gamma rays Very penetrating rays emitted by radioactive substances.

gantry Also called gantry assembly. A frame housing the equipment used in CT scans.

half-life The time required for half of the atoms in a radioactive substance to decay into other elements.

isotope One of two or more nuclides that are chemically the same but differ in mass number because their nuclei have different numbers of neutrons.

mammography A radiologic screening examination of the breasts.

metabolically active Using oxygen to burn fuel to produce energy. Some cell groups, such as those in the brain and muscles, are more metabolically active than others.

neutron An atomic particle with no charge and a mass slightly larger than that of a proton.

nuclear medicine The medical science that uses radioactive isotopes to diagnose and treat diseases.

nucleus The central core of a body or object.

nuclide A nuclear species with a certain atomic mass and number.

photon A particle with no mass and no charge.

piezoelectric effect In ultrasound, the conversion of one form of energy into another, such as the conversion of electrical energy into mechanical energy.

positron A particle of mass smaller than an atom and with a charge equal to that of an electron (but of positive charge).

proton An atomic particle identical to the nucleus of the hydrogen atom; the positively charged unit of the nuclear mass.

radioactivity The property of electrons splitting off from an atomic particle.

radionuclide An isotope of natural or artificial origin that emits exhibits radioactivity.

radiopharmaceutical A chemical preparation that contains radioactive atoms and is used as a diagnostic (or therapeutic) agent.

radium A rare radioactive element.

scintigram In nuclear medicine, a recording of the radioactivity emitted by a radionuclide in an organism or an organ system.

seismology The study of earthquakes and related phenomena.

tomography A general word meaning thin slice or thin section.

transducer In ultrasound, a hand-held device that sends and receives a sound wave signal. It changes an electrical impulse into a sound wave, receives the reflected sound wave, and converts it back into electrical energy for diagnostic purposes.

voxel Each defined unit of size of an element being scanned in computerized tomography.

X-ray A form of electromagnetic radiation capable of going through solids, similar to light but of a shorter wavelength.

For More Information

ORGANIZATIONS AND JOURNALS

American Roentgen Ray Society
American Journal of Roentgenology
44211 Slatestone Court
Leesburg, VA 20176-5109
(800) 438-2777
Web site: http://www.arrs.org

Radiological Society of North America, Inc.
Radiology
820 Jorie Boulevard
Oak Brook, IL 60523-2251
(630) 571-2670
Web site: http://www.rsna.org

WEB SITES

Due to the changing nature of Internet links, the Rosen Publishing Group, Inc., has developed an online list of Web sites related to the subject of this book. This site is updated regularly. Please use this link to access the list:

http://www.rosenlinks.com/lfm/remi/

For Further Reading

Arnold, Nick. *Medicine Now and Into the Future.* London: Thameside Press, 1999.

Brain, Marshall. *How Stuff Works.* New York: Hungry Minds, Inc., 2001.

Dowswell, Paul. *Medicine* (Great Inventions). Crystal Lake, IL: Heinemann Library, 2001.

Kevles, Bettyann H. *Naked to the Bone: Medical Imaging in the Twentieth Century.* New Brunswick, NJ: Rutgers University Press, 1997.

Macauly, David. *The New Way Things Work.* Boston: Houghton Mifflin Company, 1998.

McClafferty, Carla. *Head Bone's Connected to the Neck Bones.* New York: Farrar, Straus and Giroux, 2001.

Park, Steve. *Medicine.* London: Dorling Kindersley, 1995.

Yount, Lisa. *Medical Technology.* New York: Facts on File, 1998.

Bibliography

Barkovich, A. James, M.D. *Pediatric Neuroimaging*, 3rd ed. Philadelphia: Lippincott Williams & Wilkins, 2000.

Haller, Jack O., M.D., and Thomas L. Slovis, M.D. *Pediatric Radiology*, 2nd ed. New York: Springer-Verlag, 1995.

Lyon, G. Reid, and Judith M. Rumsey, eds. *Neuroimaging: A Window to the Neurological Foundations of Learning.* Baltimore: Paul H. Brooks Publishing Co., Inc., 1996.

Mettler, Fred A., M.D., and Milton Guiberteau, M.D. *Essentials of Nuclear Medicine Imaging*, 4th ed. Philadelphia: W.B. Saunders Company, 1998.

Mettler, Fred A., M.D., Milton J. Guiberteau, M.D., Carolyn M Voss, M.D., and Christopher Urbina, M.D. *Primary Care Radiology*. Philadelphia: W. B. Saunders Company, 2000.

Novelline, Robert A., M.D., ed. *The Radiologic Clinics of North America*, Vol. 37, No. 5. Philadelphia: W. B. Saunders Company, September 1999.

Squire, Lucy F., M.D., and Robert A. Novelline, M.D. *Fundamentals of Radiology*, 4th ed. Cambridge, MA: Harvard University Press, 1988.

Index

Credits

ABOUT THE AUTHOR

Barbara Moe has a bachelor of science degree in nursing from the College of Nursing and Health, University of Cincinnati; a Master of Science degree in nursing from Ohio State University; and a Master of Social Work degree from the University of Denver. She has written many books for the Rosen Publishing Group, including *Coping with Eating Disorders*, *Coping with Chronic Illness*, *Coping with Tourette Syndrome and Tic Disorders*, and *Everything You Need to Know About Migraines and Other Headaches*.

PHOTO CREDITS

Cover © V.C.L/FPG International; cover inset (front and back), p. 1 © PhotoDisc, Getty Images; folio banners © EyeWire; p. 4 © Doug Martin/PhotoResearchers; pp. 6, 44–45 © Custom Medical Stock Photo; p. 7 © SuperStock; p. 9 © AP/Wide World Photos; p. 14 © T. Bannor/CMSP; pp. 18, 28 © Michael English M.D/CMSP; p. 21 © B.S.I.P/CMSP; pp. 22–23 © J. Smith/CMSP; pp. 30–31 © Wellcome/PhotoResearchers; p. 33 © Berndt/CMSP; p. 34 © Mason Morfit/FPG; p. 37 © Larry Mulvehill/PhotoResearchers; p. 40 © R. D'Amico/CMSP; p. 47 © NMSB/CMSP; p. 49 © Sebastian Gollings/SuperStock; p. 50 © Lonni Duka/Index Stock Imagery.

SERIES DESIGN

Evelyn Horovicz